WOMEN
OF THE
BIBLE

John Green

DOVER PUBLICATIONS, INC.
Mineola, New York

Note

Their names have long been familiar to any reader of the Bible: Eve, Sarah, Lot's Wife, Bathsheba, Ruth, Jezebel, and many more. From pious and prayerful to devious and dissolute, the women of the Bible are human types, whose virtues and vices, recorded in the ancient biblical texts, have become part of the fabric of Western culture. They're all here: saints and harlots, faithful mothers and wives, queens, sorceresses, concubines, business women. Each is rendered in a characteristic scene or locale—in detailed, historically accurate illustrations that are educational and informative, as well as fun to color. Brief captions describe the scene and give relevant facts about the woman's role in biblical history.

List of Illustrations

Bibliographical Note

Women of the Bible is a new work, first published by Dover Publications, Inc., in 2007.

International Standard Book Number

ISBN-13: 978-0-486-45193-0
ISBN-10: 0-486-45193-3

Manufactured in the United States by Courier Corporation
45193302
www.doverpublications.com

In the Garden of Eden, the serpent tempts Eve to eat the forbidden fruit of the Tree of Knowledge.

Afterward, she and Adam are cast out of the Garden by the Lord.

1

Sarah was the wife of Abraham, founder of the House of Israel. When Sarah was unable to bear a child, Sarah asked her servant Hagar to bear one for her. After Hagar had given birth, however, she became arrogant and prideful. Sarah complained about her to Abraham.

Finally, Sarah could stand it no more, and commanded Hagar to take her son, Ishmael, and go forth into the desert. Hagar and Ishmael were later rescued by an angel of the Lord.

When the Lord rained fire and brimstone on the evil city of Sodom, Lot and his family were instructed to flee and not look back. Lot's wife, however, could not resist a last gaze at the burning city, and, for her disobedience, was turned into a pillar of salt.

Rebekah offers water to the servant of Abraham, who has come to the well in search of a suitable wife for his master's son, Isaac. The servant is impressed by Rebekah's kindness and generosity. Soon after, Isaac and Rebekah are married.

Jacob, grandson of Abraham, meets Rachel, a young and beautiful shepherdess, at the well at Haran. He later asks her father Laban for Rachel's hand.

6

When Prince Shechem lays eyes on Dinah, daughter of Jacob and Leah, he falls in love with her instantly. However, his bold and aggressive actions toward Dinah bring the wrath of Dinah's brothers on Shechem and his people.

The wife of Potiphar, an Egyptian official, loves Joseph, a young Hebrew slave in her household. When Joseph rejects her advances, the wife tells lies to her husband and causes Joseph to be thrown into prison.

Jochebed, mother of Moses, hides her baby in the reeds along the Nile to protect him from Pharaoh's soldiers, who have orders to kill all male Hebrew children.

Shortly afterward, Pharaoh's daughter and her attendants, having come to the river to bathe, find the baby Moses in his little boat. The Egyptian princess decides to raise him as her own.

Moses meets Zipporah, daughter of Jethro, when she and her sisters bring their flock of sheep to the well. Moses marries Zipporah, but as Moses becomes a great leader, he and his wife spend little time together.

After helping her brother Moses lead the Israelites across the parted Red Sea (Sea of Reeds), saving them from the wrath of Pharaoh's soldiers, Miriam dances and plays the timbrel to celebrate.

Rahab, an innkeeper in the city of Jericho, hides two Jewish spies belonging to Joshua's army, which is preparing to attack the city. She helps them because she believes in the god of the Israelites. Later, when Jericho falls, Rahab and her family are spared because of her assistance to Joshua's men.

A counselor and judge in times of peace, Deborah became an inspiring leader in a time of war. Here she instructs the military man Barak to lead the Israelites in battle against the Canaanites, who had long oppressed her people.

Delilah, a beautiful but treacherous Philistine woman loved by Samson, finally persuades the Hebrew warrior to reveal the secret of his great strength. Samson admits that his power lies in his long hair. After he falls asleep, Delilah summons a Philistine to cut off Samson's luxuriant locks, thereby robbing him of his might.

Ruth, a Moabite woman, comes to the attention of Boaz, a wealthy Hebrew landowner, when he sees her gleaning grain in his fields. Impressed by her beauty and hard work, Boaz becomes her protector, showering favors upon her and helping her in many little ways.

After a time Ruth marries Boaz, who is actually a distant kinsman. From their union comes a little boy, Obed. His birth marks the founding of the House of David. Here Naomi, Ruth's beloved mother-in-law, takes care of the baby.

After her fervent prayers to the Lord to help her conceive a child, Hannah gives birth to Samuel, who will grow up to be one of the great Hebrew prophets. In this picture Hannah takes Samuel to the temple to be educated as a priest.

Michal, daughter of King Saul, fell in love with young David, who had vanquished the Philistine giant, Goliath. Saul, however, jealous of David's prowess, sought to kill the young Israelite. Here Michal helps David escape from her murderous father.

Abigail is the wife of Nabal, a drunken selfish man possessed of large herds of sheep and goats. When he denies David and his men the food to which they are justly entitled for protecting his property, David prepares to destroy Nabal and his household. Abigail takes it upon herself to provide the food, thereby averting disaster. After Nabal dies, Abigail becomes one of David's wives.

Late in life, King Saul, a weary and fear-ridden old man, visits the Witch of Endor, a sorceress. The witch summons the spirit of the dead prophet Samuel, who foretells Saul's downfall and death. The next day, Saul is beheaded by the Philistines.

One evening, King David spies on the beautiful Bathsheba in her bath. Desiring her for his own, David arranges for her husband Uriah, a soldier, to be sent to the front lines of a fierce battle. After Uriah is killed, King David makes Bathsheba his wife.

Widow of Judah's sons Onan and Er, Tamar dons a disguise and waits for her father-in-law to pass by. She plans to deceive him into giving her the children she has always wanted. She later becomes mother of twins by Judah.

The Queen of Sheba comes from her kingdom in Arabia to visit King Solomon in Jerusalem. Her lavish caravan, laden with gold, jewels, silver, and precious spices, is recorded as one of the most impressive ever to enter the city. It is thought that one of the reasons for her visit may have been to work out trade agreements with Solomon.

The strong-willed daughter of a king of Zidonia, Jezebel convinced her husband, King Ahab, to adopt pagan customs and worship the god Baal.

She was a bad influence on her husband. For this the Hebrew prophet Elijah denounced her to Ahab, after which she and Elijah became bitter enemies.

When the Israelite town of Bethulia was besieged by the Assyrian general Holofernes, a young Jewish widow named Judith sneaked into the general's tent and plied him with wine. After Holofernes fell asleep, Judith cut off his head, and took it back to Bethulia, where she presented it to the people. The next day, the Israelites defeated the enemy.

Esther, a young Jewish woman, is chosen from among many to be wife of King Ahasuerus of Persia. When his evil prime minister, Haman, orders the massacre of all Jews, Esther pleads with the king to spare her people. He does so and executes Haman instead. Esther's courageous deed gave rise to the Feast of Purim.

Mother of John the Baptist, Elizabeth is the first to greet her cousin Mary as the mother of the Messiah. Having been made aware of the great role Mary is destined to play as the mother of Jesus, Elizabeth tells her cousin: "Blessed art thou among women, and blessed is the fruit of thy womb."

Since there was no room in the inn at Bethlehem, Mary has given birth to Jesus in the stable of the inn. Wrapped in swaddling clothes in His little cradle, the Christ child is an object of wonder and adoration for the shepherds and wise men who have come to gaze upon Him.

After Christ cast seven demons out of her body, Mary Magdalen became one of His most devoted disciples. Following the crucifixion, she is the first to see the empty tomb and to witness the risen Christ.